MW00914684

# *Fatherhood*

# *- Quotes -*

*Thinking of you on*
## *Father's Day*
*And Every Day*

***For My Departed Father,***
*Who I miss*

***And My Brother,***
*Who makes it easier for me*

# *Table of Contents*

*Imagine your father picking up this **gift book** from you every now and then and reading a few passages.*

*He smiles, maybe his lips tighten stoically and he looks like he's trying not to get choked up.*

***He thinks of you** and gets the thousand-yard stare for a few moments.*

*This is why this book was published.*

*It was written to celebrate fathers and fatherhood. It is divided into sections for easy reference and paced throughout with ornamentation and caricature to **avoid that dreaded "WALL OF TEXT"** look. The paperback, doubly so!*

*The people quoted were not picked for any reason other than whether or not their words might make an impact on the reader. I will be honest, as a father myself there were times when I was a little emotional compiling this. If it were otherwise, either the quotes weren't worthy or maybe I wouldn't be as much of a father as I hope I am!*

*The sections run from heartwarming to hilarious.*

*There are some for fathers of sons, and some for daughters. There are some about "non-biological" fathers and even a few about grandfathers.*

*From philosophers and writers to artists and pop culture icons.*

*Some are from fathers themselves and some others singing their praises, but all of them are sincere reflections on the fathers we depend on.*

*Share the love.*

*Let's get started here. With the…*

# Top 40 Picks from This Collection

### Al Roker
*One of the greatest lessons I learned from my dad was to make sure your children know that you love them.*

### Al Unser
*Dad taught me everything I know. Unfortunately, he didn't teach me everything he knows.*

### Aldous Huxley
*Sons have always a rebellious wish to be disillusioned by that which charmed their fathers.*

### Andrew Galasetti
*Papas should be loving their children so much that they cry when they gone. That's what papas is supposed to do.*

### Antoine François Prévost d'Exiles
*The heart of a father is the masterpiece of nature.*

### Asa Don Brown
*Fatherhood is the greatest education a man can ever receive.*

### Ben Fountain
*Much of life, fatherhood included, is the story of knowledge acquired too late: If only I'd known then what I know now, how much smarter, abler, stronger, I would have been. But nothing really prepares you for kids, for the swells of emotion that roll through your chest like the rumble of boulders tumbling downhill, nor for the all-enveloping labor of it, the sheer mulish endurance you need for the six or seven hundred discrete tasks that have to be done each and every day.*

### Carl Veraha
*I felt something I had never felt before, a mixture of fear and pride. I liked it. This was fatherhood. The biggest mistake anyone could make, and yet universally accepted. I had arrived.*

### Charles Kettering
*Every father should remember one day his son will follow his example, not his advice.*

### Craig D. Lounsbrough
*A father is the man who realizes that a life spent in the service of his children is the creation of a legacy so vast that it can be deeply drawn from for generations to come, but it will never be emptied by any who come to it.*

### David Frost
*Having one child makes you a parent. Having two kids makes you a referee.*

### Eugene Levy
*Don't think you're better than your kid. Your kids usually have ideas that are better than yours that you may not understand.*

### Fela Durotoye
*Real Fathers are men of integrity & honour. Their word is their bond.*

### George Bernard Shaw
*Parentage is a very important profession, but no test of fitness for it is ever imposed in the interest of the children.*

### Gloria Naylor
*Old as she was, she still missed her daddy sometimes.*

### George Herbert
*One father is more than a hundred schoolmasters.*

**Gregory David Roberts**
*Nothing ever fits the palm so perfectly, or feels so right, or inspires so much protective instinct as the hand of a child.*

**Hanya Yanagihara**
*I thought those thoughts all men think when a woman tells them she's pregnant: What would the baby look like? Would I like it? Would I love it? And then, more crushingly: fatherhood. With all its responsibilities and fulfillments and tedium and possibilities for failure.*

**Henry Ward Beecher**
*We never know the love of a parent till we become parents ourselves.*

**J. Sterling**
*… anyone could father a child, but a real man chooses to be a dad.*

**Jim Gaffigan**
*There should be a children's song: 'If you're happy and you know it, keep it to yourself and let dad sleep.'*

**Joan Ambu**
*Being a father is a choice. Staying true to fatherhood is a duty.*

**Lady Gaga**
*I love my Daddy. My Daddy's everything. I hope I can find a man that will treat me as good as my dad.*

**Liam Neeson**
*I try to be a hard boiled sometimes. My kids see right through it. I'm acting. It's always, 'When I say you'll be back at 11, that means 11, not 11.15. Do you hear me!?' Then, 'Yeah, Dad.'*

**Marinela Reka**
*Being a daddy's girl is like having a permanent armor for the rest of your life.*

**Mekael Shane**
*Sons are born to make their fathers better men.*

**Oliver Hudson**
*Father or stepfather - those are just titles to me. They don't mean anything.*

**Orson Scott Card**
*I hope I am remembered by my children as a good father.*

**Pam Brown**
*Dads are most ordinary men turned by love into heroes, adventures, story-tellers, and singers of songs.*

**Phil McGraw**
*My dad used to say, 'You wouldn't worry so much about what people thought about you if you knew how seldom they did.'*

**Rick Riordan**
*A father should do more - a father should give more to his children than he takes.*

**Ron Baratono**
*The finest compliment a man can receive from a woman, is to be told he's a wonderful father.*

**Ken Norton**
*Of all the titles I've been privileged to have, 'Dad' has always been the best.*

**Steve Martin**
*A father carries pictures where his money used to be.*

**Sunday Adelaja**
*Fatherhood is a man's main goal and appointed purpose in life*

**Susan Gale**
*A father's smile has been known to light up a child's entire day.*

**Tim Allen**
*Dad needs to show an incredible amount of respect and humor and friendship toward his mate so the kids understand their parents are sexy, they're fun, they do things together, they're best friends. Kids learn by example. If I respect Mom, they're going to respect Mom.*

**Unknown**
*A little girl giggles when she is denied an ice cream by her mother.  She knows daddy will get her some later.*

**Unknown**
*A father holds his daughter's hand for a short while, but he holds her heart forever.*

**Walter M. Schirra**
*You don't raise heroes, you raise sons. And if you treat them like sons, they'll turn out to be heroes, even if it's just in your own eyes.*

**Zadie Smith**
*You don't have favourites among your children, but you do have allies.*

# *Heartwarming*

### *Al Roker*
*One of the greatest lessons I learned from my dad was to make sure your children know that you love them.*

### *Ama H. Vanniarachchy*
*A father's tears and fears are unseen, his love is unexpressed, but his care and protection remains as a pillar of strength throughout our lives.*

### *Ben Fountain*
*Much of life, fatherhood included, is the story of knowledge acquired too late: If only I'd known then what I know now, how much smarter, abler, stronger, I would have been. But nothing really prepares you for kids, for the swells of emotion that roll through your chest like the rumble of boulders tumbling downhill, nor for the all-enveloping labor of it, the sheer mulish endurance you need for the six or seven hundred discrete tasks that have to be done each and every day.*

### *Amish Tripathi*
*A man does not become a father merely through his body. A man earns the privilege of fatherhood with his protection, his care, his ability to provide. A man earns fatherhood by being worthy of emulation. A man earns fatherhood through love.*

### *Andrea Bocelli*
*Fatherhood is a very natural thing; it's not something that shakes up my life but rather it enriches it.*

### *Andrew Galasetti*
*Papas should be loving their children so much that they cry when they gone. That's what papas is supposed to do.*

**Andrew Pettegree**
*Like many men who experience fatherhood relatively late in life, Martin Luther was a devoted parent. Luther wrote his children letters of touching intensity, patiently converting the joys of the Christian life into a language of storytelling fit for the very young. A home with children brought out the best in Luther in a way that theological disputation patently did not.*

**Angelina Jolie**
*And my dad, you're a great actor but you're a better father.*

**Angelo Patri**
*The father who would taste the essence of his fatherhood must turn back from the plane of his experience, take with him the fruits of his journey and begin again beside his child, marching step by step over the same old road.*

**Anonymous**
*Fatherhood became my ideology.*

**Anthony Doerr**
*There is a humility of being a father to someone so powerful, as if he were only a narrow conduit for another, greater thing. That's how it feels right now, he thinks, kneeling beside her, rinsing her hair: as though his love for his daughter will outstrip the limits of his body. The walls could fall away, even the whole city, and the brightness of that feeling would not wane.*

**Antoine François Prévost d'Exiles**
*The heart of a father is the masterpiece of nature.*

**Arne Duncan**
*There was nothing more important I could do than be supportive as a dad.*

### Asa Don Brown
*As fathers, we should have a desire to be active participants in our children's lives.*

*ᏰᎦ   ᏽᏮ*

*As a father, we need to actively listen.*

### Ben Fountain
*Much of life, fatherhood included, is the story of knowledge acquired too late: if only I'd known then what I know now, how much smarter, abler, stronger, I would have been. But nothing really prepares you for kids, for the swells of emotion that roll through your chest like the rumble of boulders tumbling downhill, nor for the all-enveloping labor of it, the sheer mulish endurance you need for the six or seven hundred discrete tasks that have to be done each and every day. Such a small person! Not much bigger than a loaf of bread at first, yet it takes so much to keep the whole enterprise going. Logistics, skills, materiel; the only way we really learn is by figuring it out as we go along, and even then it changes on us every day, so we're always improvising, which is a fancy way of saying that we're doing things we technically don't know how to do.*

### Billie Joe Armstrong
*I'm a father. It isn't just my life any more. I don't want my kid finding bottles in the house or seeing his father completely smashed.*

### Buffalo Bill
*But the love of adventure was in father's blood.*

### C.J. Tudor
*Wise man. Kids from the moment they're born, they fill your heart with love…and terror. Especially little girls. You want to protect them from everything. And they you can't, you feel like you've failed as a father. You've saved yourself a lot of pain by not having children.*

### Carl Veraha
*I felt something I had never felt before, a mixture of fear and pride. I liked it. This was fatherhood. The biggest mistake anyone could make, and yet universally accepted. I had arrived.*

### Chimamanda Ngozi Adichie
*A father is as much a verb as a mother.*

### Craig D. Lounsbrough
*The call of fatherhood is in fact a call of sacrifice, not in some heroic sense where a father is lifted high on some glowing pedestal with all of his sacrifices held up to the awe of those around him. Rather, it is a call that will cost him all that he has, that will be absent of accolades, where rewards will be sparse, and where he will someday find himself having spent all, but in the spending have gained everything. And this is the glory of fatherhood.*

### Chris Hemsworth
*I think [parenthood] brings out the child in all of us. That's what's so beautiful. It reminds you of the fascination you had with things, and how you can spend hours just being with someone. It's amazing.*

### Chris Pratt
*I've gotten to jump out of helicopters and do daring stunts and play baseball in a professional stadium, but none of them mean anything compared to being somebody's daddy.*

### Christopher Meloni
*The surprising thing about fatherhood was finding my inner mush. Now I want to share it with the world.*

### Cindy Crawford
*Watching your husband become a father is really sexy and wonderful.*

### Connie Kerbs
*Motherhood (and fatherhood) is one of the most important, while at the same time being one of the most long-time, unappreciated roles we may ever find ourselves in. Add to that, it seems at times to be taken as much for granted by our society at large, as by the developing young we pour our all into. Quality parenting is also wrought with joy and satisfaction at every turn, being one of the most rewarding, and fulfilling experiences we have the opportunity to know in this thing we call the human condition.*

### Cormac McCarthy
*They slept huddled together in the rank quilts in the dark and the cold. He held the boy close to him. So thin. My heart, he said. My heart.*

### Craig D. Lounsbrough
*The father who has selflessly poured himself into the life of his children may leave no other monument than that of his children. But as for a life well lived, no other monument is necessary.*

### Dr. Tony Beizaee
*When you learn to live unselfishly in united adoration of your beloved family, you have fulfilled the art of Fatherhood.*

### David Beckham
*In my career, there's many things I've won and many things I've achieved, but for me, my greatest achievement is my children and my family.*

### David Bowie
*I'm very at ease, and I like it. I never thought I would be such a family-oriented guy I didn't think that was part of my makeup. But somebody said that as you get older you become the person you always should have been, and I feel that's happening to me. I'm rather surprised at who I am, because I'm actually like my dad!*

### David Cassidy
*As a father, I do everything my dad didn't do. My son Beau's birth changed my life.*

### David Harewood
*Fatherhood is a joy. I feel very lucky to have a family. It gives you a perspective on things.*

### Debasish Mridha
*I love you Daddy, not because you always loved my, because you are always living inside of me as an inspiration of my being.*

### DeForest Kelley
*The most important influence in my childhood was my father.*

### Dimitri the Stoneheart
*A father doesn't tell you that he loves you. He shows you.*

### Don DeLillo
*He found his cigar smoldering in an ashtray on the liquor cabinet and he fired it up again. The aroma gave him a sense of robust health. He smelled well-being, long life, even placid fatherhood, somewhere, in the burning leaf.*

### Dwyane Wade
*Fatherhood is the best thing that could happen to me, and I'm just glad I can share my voice.*

### Emile Gaboriau
*A father is the one friend upon whom we can always rely.*

### George Strait
*Daddies don't just love their children every now and then, it's a love without end.*

### Hendrith Vanlon Smith, Jr.
*Fathers have unique value, and we are irreplaceable in the hearts of our children.*

*The importance of fatherhood is indisputable. And children always reach for their fathers.*

### Henry Ward Beecher
*We never know the love of a parent till we become parents ourselves.*

### Howard W. Hunter
*One of the greatest things a father can do for his children is to love their mother.*

### Jim DeMint
*One of the greatest titles in the world is parent, and one of the biggest blessings in the world is to be one.*

### Jim Valvano
*My father gave me the greatest gift anyone could give another person: He believed in me.*

### John Green
*A father's love still travels on after he's gone. A treasure hidden in the hearts of his children.*

**John Legend**
*It's a different kind of love. It's very pure. It's unconditional.*

**Ken Norton**
*Of all the titles I've been privileged to have, 'Dad' has always been the best.*

**Kevin Costner**
*It almost seemed impossible to love the first [child] any more than you loved them. And then suddenly the second one comes, and you think there's so much room for love. There's so much room.*

**LeBron James**
*My favourite thing about being a father is just seeing my kids grow and do some of the same things that I did when I was a kid, man.*

**Len Filppu**
*When faced with first time fatherhood at the age of 49, I didn't know whether to celebrate with champagne… or hemlock.*

**Melvina Young**
*Dad hugs are strong hugs that can say so many things, like 'I've got you. I'm always right here. And I'll always love you.'*

**Michael Bublé**
*Fatherhood is the greatest thing that could ever happen. You can't explain it until it happens; it's like telling somebody what water feels like before they've ever swam in it.*

**Mike Myers**
*Anyone who tells you fatherhood is the greatest thing that can happen to you, they are understating it.*

### Ron Baratono
*The finest compliment a man can receive from a woman, is to be told he's a wonderful father.*

### Ryan Reynolds
*It's amazing that you can be that exhausted and that happy at the same time.*

### Seth Meyers
*It is so embarrassing how I went from a person who did not care about anyone's children. Then you have them, and you brag about the same stuff that you never cared about. And you tell people, 'He's got four teeth,' like they care.*

### Tom Daley
*My dad was an incredibly brave man, completely dedicated to his family, with a love for all of us. If I can be half the dad he was to me then that will be an achievement in itself.*

### Unknown
*Dad: A son's first hero, a daughter's first love.*

# *Hilarious*

**Alan Cumming**
*My mum always told me I was precious, while my dad always told me I was worthless. I think that's a good grounding for a balanced life.*

**Al Unser**
*Dad taught me everything I know. Unfortunately, he didn't teach me everything he knows.*

**Ann Napolitano**
*Fatherhood, is for him, one jolt of terror after another.*

**Ann Richards**
*I have always had the feeling I could do anything and my dad told me I could. I was in college before I found out he might be wrong.*

**August Strindberg**
*That is the thankless position of the father in the family - the provider for all, and the enemy of all.*

**Barbara Claypole White**
*Fatherhood doesn't come with an expiration date.*

**Barry White**
*I kept my babies fed. I could have dumped them, but I didn't. I decided that whatever trip I was on, they were going with me. You're looking at a real daddy.*

**Ben Marcus**
*The task of being right is a task the father perfects over time.*

### Bertrand Russell
*The place of the father in the modern suburban family is a very small one, particularly if he plays golf.*

### Ben Sirach
*A daughter is a treasure and a cause of sleeplessness.*

### Bob Odenkirk
*My daughter got me a World's Best Dad mug. So, we know she's sarcastic.*

### Bono
*Overcoming my dad telling me that I could never amount to anything is what has made me the megalomaniac that you see today.*

### Broderick Crawford
*My father was always telling himself no one was perfect, not even my mother.*

### Bryan Pulsifer
*A daughter can lead to baldness, but the remainder of the road is just as smooth.*

### Bubba Watson
*My dad taught me to be a leader or a follower, and he said follower ain't fun. So I want to be the leader of Bubba Watson.*

### Cameron Diaz
*My dad always used to tell me that if they challenge you to an after-school fight, tell them you won't wait-you can kick their ass right now.*

### Cat Deeley
*The only time I ever look good dancing is if I'm next to my dad at a wedding.*

### Chely Wright
*I recruited my dad to be my bass player and fired him on several occasions. He stayed on as a bus driver.*

### Chris O'Donnell
*I am an obsessive garage cleaner - my wife and the neighbors make fun of me. I remember that my father was the same way, and now when I'm out there unearthing things in the garage, I realize I am becoming my dad!*

### Christie Hefner
*No, I never thought about my father's money as my money.*

### Claire Cullen
*So, key things to remember. If it's bigger than you, run. If it's got wheels, get out of its way. Fatherhood is tough but worth it, or so I hear. No matter what a fox tells you, they don't want to be your friend.*

### Connor Garrett
*I'll tell you a secret: Every adult was a kid once and is learning how to be a parent along the way.*

### Curtis Stone
*Now that I'm a dad, I'm practicing what I call 'one- handed cooking,' because I've got something more important in my other arm. I'm whipping up lots of frittatas and omelets.*

### Dan Pearce
*Saturday mornings, I've learned, are a great opportunity for kids to sneak into your bed, fall back asleep, and kick you in the face.*

### Dave Attell
*When you're young, you think your dad is Superman. Then you grow up, and you realize he's just a regular guy who wears a cape.*

### David Crystal
*As I get older and I get a few more years experience I become more like Dad, you know, King Lear.*

### Dax Shepard
*I rescind my early statement, 'I could never fall in love with a girl who regularly poops her pants.' I hadn't met my daughter yet.*

### David Frost
*Having one child makes you a parent. Having two kids makes you a referee.*

### Delano Johnson
*Fathers are no longer men, most are only boys who pretend.*

### Dimebag Darrell
*The worst advice I ever received from my dad was to play by the book.*

### Eva Green
*I'm worried because of my mother, she's going to see my performance and she's quite hard. She's going to see me naked. And my Dad, woah. Yeah, they're going to see me like a woman, you know?*

### Frank Butler
*When I was 18, I thought my father was pretty dumb. After a while when I got to be 21, I was amazed to find out how much he'd learned in three years.*

### Fred Allen
*My father never raised his hand to any one of his children, except in self-defense.*

### Gary Vaynerchuk
*People who build family businesses are not classically trained. They have to deal with an enormous amount of politics. You think corporate politics are tough? Go work for your dad or your mom.*

### Glenn Frey
*I'm just as insufferable and useless as every other dad is. The dynamic never changes, no matter what you do for a living.*

### Fredrik Backman
*He just didn't know how to prepare himself for fatherhood. He had asked for some sort of manual.*

### Harmon Killebrew
*My father used to play with my brother and me in the yard. Mother would come out and say, 'You're tearing up the grass' 'We're not raising grass,' Dad would reply. 'We're raising boys.'*

### Harrison Ford
*I love the comic opportunities that come up in the context of a father-son relationship.*

### Harry S. Truman
*My father was not a failure. After all, he was the father of a president of the United States.*

### Henny Youngman
*My dad was the town drunk. Most of the time that's not so bad but New York City?*

### James Breakwell
*Four-year-old: Tell me a scary story! Me: One time little people popped out of your mom, and they never stopped asking questions. Four-year-old: Why?*

### Jason Ritter
*Even if I tried to be my dad, it would be a mediocre, slightly embarrassing version.*

### Jeff Lindsay
*It had been my experience that fatherhood was mostly a matter of suffering the insufferable, tolerating the intolerable, and changing diapers.*

### Jerry Seinfeld
*You can tell what was the best year of your father's life, because they seem to freeze that clothing style and ride it out.*

### Jim Gaffigan
*There should be a children's song: 'If you're happy and you know it, keep it to yourself and let dad sleep.*

*Now that I am a father myself, I know that powerlessness is the defining characteristic of fatherhood. This begins with the pregnancy. Men spend their whole lives being active. We evolved as hunters. "Me get job, me get girl, me get girl pregnant. Now me shut mouth and wait for girl to tell me what to do." As expectant fathers, we become silent spectators. Passive participants in a series of external events over which we have zero control.*

*Raising kids may be a thankless job but at least the pay sucks.*

### John Lithgow
*I'm a fun father, but not a good father. The hard decisions always went to my wife.*

### John Wilmot
*Before I got married I had six theories about raising children; now, I have six children and no theories.*

### Jonathan Tropper
*If there's a perk to having such a fucked up father, it's that he's in no position to judge.*

### José Saramago
*It just isn't possible for you to ask me all the questions, or for me to give you all the answers.*

### Lex Croucher
*You know fathers aren't always right just by virtue of being fathers.*

### Liam Neeson
*I try to be a hard boiled sometimes. My kids see right through it. I'm acting. It's always, 'When I say you'll be back at 11, that means 11, not 11.15. Do you hear me!?' Then, 'Yeah, Dad.'*

### Lou Brock
*When I was a kid, I used to imagine animals running under my bed. I told my dad, and he solved the problem quickly. He cut the legs off the bed.*

### Lloyd Alexander
*...alas, raising a young lady is a mystery even beyond an enchanter's skill.*

### Mark R. Brand
*For every guy who loves being a dad, there's another who realizes too late that he's created something his wife loves more than him.*

**Mark Twain**
*When I was a boy of 14, my father was so ignorant, I could hardly stand to have the old man around. But when I got to be 21, I was astonished at how much the old man had learned in seven years.*

**Melanie Fiona**
*My dad still calls me and makes sure I'm taking my vitamins.*

**Michael Crummey**
*From what I have seen of the world, Reverend, motherhood is a certainty, but fatherhood is a subject of debate.*

**Michael Lewis**
*Memory loss is the key to human reproduction. If you remembered what new parenthood was actually like you wouldn't go around lying to people about how wonderful it* ... *it twice.*

**Prince Charles**
*Father told me that if I ever met a lady in a dress like yours, I must look her straight in the eyes.*

**Ray Romano**
*If my father had hugged me even once, I'd be an accountant right now.*

**Raymond Chandler**
*A man who indulges in parenthood for the first time at the age of fifty-four deserves all he gets.*

**Reed Markham**
*Being a great father is like shaving. No matter how good you shaved today, you have to do it again tomorrow.*

**Rich Sommer**
*I've certainly had less practice at fatherhood than I have at acting, but in fatherhood, at least my failures are private!*

**Ryan Reynolds**
*Nothing better than spending an entire morning staring into my baby daughter's eyes, whispering, 'I can't do this.'*

ᏬᏫ

*On our 6 a.m. walk, my daughter asked where the moon goes each morning. I let her know it's in heaven visiting Daddy's freedom.*

**Shahrukh Khan**
*Whenever I fail as a father or husband... a toy and a diamond always works.*

**Sharon Stone**
*I was lucky to have my dad in my life. As crazy as things got, I always had him to put his hand on my shoulder.*

**Steve Martin**
*A father carries pictures where his money used to be.*

**Tim Russert**
*The older I get, the smarter my father seems to get.*

**Unknown**
*A father is someone you look up to no matter how tall you grow.*

**Zidrou**
*I think any dad who slices a large pickle in two for their kids' sandwich is always a good dad!*

# *Inspirational*

### *A.K. Kuykendall*
*Son, we are all products of operant conditioning. By daring to think outside the box, you'll be judged. Stay the course. Heightened cognizance is meaningful only when freely sought out and discovered. Not when it is incrementally spoon-fed to you throughout your lifetime.*

### **Adrian Leslie Lobo**
*The word "FATHER" holds significant value in the bible for a reason… Family. Provider. Aftermath. Teacher. Trusted. Protector. Hidden Fighter. Essence of Living. Root to your origin. Remember; You are the reason why this world exists.*

### **Anonymous**
*In another of his most famous essays, Montaigne argued that to philosophise is to learn to die. I learned how to die with fatherhood. From the day Tito was born, I was completely cancelled out by him. I lost my will. I ceased to exist. Only a dead person can cease to exist. If philosophising is learning to die, then fatherhood is the philosophy of the ordinary man, the philosophy of the poor in spirit, the philosophy of the masses.*

### **Asa Don Brown**
*Fatherhood is the greatest education a man can ever receive.*

### **Barack Obama**
*It's the courage to raise a child that makes you a father.*

### Brad Paisley
*Looking back all I can say about all the things he did for me is I hope I'm at least half the dad that he didn't have to be.*

### Brad Pitt
*Fatherhood is the best thing I ever did. It changes your perspective. You can write a book, you can make a movie, you can paint a painting, but having kids is really the most extraordinary thing I have taken on.*

### C.S. Lewis
*An almost perfect relationship with his father was the earthly root of all his wisdom. From his own father, he said, he first learned that Fatherhood must be at the core of the universe.*

### Camryn Manheim
*One of my earliest memories is of my father carrying me in one arm with a picket sign in the other.*

### Dante Hall
*I would want my legacy to be that I was a great son, father, and friend.*

### Denzel Washington
*The strongest, toughest men all have compassion. They're not heartless and cold. You have to be man enough to have compassion — to care about people and about your children.*

### Doris Kearns Goodwin
*Of Teddy Roosevelt and his siblings, the author writes they were, "armed with an innate curiosity and discipline fostered by his remarkable father."*

**Eugene Levy**
*Don't think you're better than your kid. Your kids usually have ideas that are better than yours that you may not understand.*

**Fahad Basheer**
*Every man can provide provision to his children if he is committed and hardworking but a man who fails to enter into the depths of the mind of his children is not is father, but a master who owns a slave!*

**Frank Abagnale**
*We all grow up. Hopefully, we get wiser. Age brings wisdom, and fatherhood changes one's life completely.*

**Frank Bruno**
*I want to stay healthy, keep fit, eat well, keep a low profile and be a good dad.*

**Frank Pittman**
*The guys who fear becoming fathers don't understand that fathering is not something perfect men do, but something that perfects the man. The end product of child-raising is not the child but the parent.*

**Franz Kafka**
*My health is only just good enough for myself alone, not good enough for marriage, let alone fatherhood. Yet when I read your letter, I feel I could overlook even what cannot possibly be overlooked.*

**George Herbert**
*One father is more than a hundred schoolmasters.*

**George Saunders**
*He was a father. That's what a father does. Eases the burdens of those he loves.*

### Gordon Brown
*I'm a father; that's what matters most. Nothing matters more.*

### Haley Joel Osment
*My dad never told me that when you audition, you might not get the role. He wanted to wait until my first disappointment to tell me.*

### Hanif Kureishi
*My son, there may be a time when I explain these things to you, because there may be a time when I understand them.*

### Hendrith Vanlon Smith Jr.
*When I meet other men in business, I want to know what their relationship with their children is like. I think a mans role as a father says something about who he is as a businessman and the quality of leader he is.*

### Henri J.M. Nouwen
*You're called to become a father who can welcome his children home without asking them any questions and without wanting anything from them in return. Most people around you don't need you to be a good friend or even a kind brother. We need you to be a father who can claim for himself the authority of true compassion. The idea of being like the old man who had nothing to lose because he had lost all, and only to give, overwhelmed me with fear. I still feel the desire to remain the son and never to grow old.*

### J. Sterling
*That anyone could father a child, but a real man chooses to be a dad.*

### Jeff Koons

*I was trying to make art that my son could look on in the future and would realize I was thinking about him very much during these times... that he can look and see my dad's thinking about me, but to also embed in these things something that is bigger than all of us.*

### Jonathan Safran Foer

*A few days after we came home from the hospital, I sent a letter to a friend, including a photo of my son and some first impressions of fatherhood. He responded, simply, 'Everything is possible again.' It was the perfect thing to write, because that was exactly how it felt. We could retell our stories and make them better, more representative or aspirational. Or we could choose to tell different stories. The world itself had another chance.*

### Joni Eareckson Tada

*There is nothing that moves a loving father's soul quite like his child's cry.*

### Josh Hatcher

*Remember the end goal You are trying to make a full grown human capable of surviving in the wild on their own. You aren't going to keep them forever. You can't make them live your life for you. You can't coddle them and do everything for them. You are preparing them to leave you. Don't lose sight of that!*

### Justin Ricklefs

*The power of a dad in a child's life is unmatched.*

### Karamo Brown

*Fatherhood is an honor, and men should be strong enough to step up to the plate.*

### Karl Ove Knausgård

*I am alive, I have my own children and with them I have tried to achieve only one aim: that they shouldn't be afraid of their father. They aren't. I know that.When I enter a room, they don't cringe, they don't look down at the floor, they don't dart off as soon as they glimpse an opportunity, no, if they look at me, it is not a look of indifference, and if there is anyone I am happy to be ignored by it is them. If there is anyone I am happy to be taken for granted by, it is them. And should they have completely forgotten I was there when they turn forty themselves, I will thank them and take a bow and accept the bouquets.*

### Ken Norton

*Of all the titles that I've been privileged to have, the title of 'dad' has always been the best.*

### Lailah Gifty Akita

*Fatherhood is sacred.*

### Lee Westwood

*The satisfaction you get when you finally beat your dad is amazing, that rush of adrenaline.*

### Leo Buscaglia

*If there is any immortality to be had among us human beings, it is certainly only in the love that we leave behind. Fathers like mine don't ever die.*

### Liam Neeson

*It's an ongoing joy being a dad.*

### Lisa Rogers
*A man's worth is measured by how he parents his children. What he gives them, what he keeps away from them, the lessons he teaches and the lessons he allows them to learn on their own.*

### Louis C.K.
*Be a dad. Don't be "Mom's Assistant".... Be a man.... Fathers have skills that they never use at home. You run a landscaping business and you can't dress and feed a four-year-old? Take it on. Spend time with your kids.... It won't take away your manhood, it will give it to you.*

### Marcus Jacob Goldman
*Some dads liken the impending birth of a child to the beginning of a great journey.*

### Martin Luther
*Now you tell me, when a father goes ahead and washes diapers or performs some other mean task for his child, and someone ridicules him as an effeminate fool, though that father is acting in the spirit just described and in Christian faith, my dear fellow you tell me, which of the two is most keenly ridiculing the other? God, with all his angels and creatures, is smiling, not because that father is washing diapers, but because he is doing so in Christian faith. Those who sneer at him and see only the task but not the faith are ridiculing God with all his creatures, as the biggest fool on earth. Indeed, they are only ridiculing themselves; with all their cleverness they are nothing but devil's fools.*

### Matthew McConaughey
*Never is a man more of a man than when he is the father of a newborn.*

### Mike Myers
*Anyone who tells you fatherhood is the greatest thing that can happen to you, they are understating it.*

### Pam Brown
*Dads are most ordinary men turned by love into heroes, adventurers, storytellers, and singers of song.*

### Paul L. Lewis
*Fatherhood is a marathon, not a sprint.*

### Pope John XXIII
*It is easier for a father to have children than for children to have a real father.*

### Prevost Abbe
*The heart of a father is the masterpiece of nature.*

### Publilius Syrus
*An angry father is most cruel towards himself.*

### Rob Kozak
*What makes a good father? A good father sets an example that his children want to follow. A good father provides for the needs of his children—both material and non-material. A good father demonstrates his love in both words and actions. A good father provides guidance in a positive fashion.*

### Rod Stewart
*I can definitely say the older I've got the better I've become at being a dad and a husband.*

### Sunday Adelaja
*Fatherhood is a man's main goal and appointed purpose in life.*

**Ta-Nehisi Coates**
*Anyone can make a baby, but it takes a man to be a father.*

**Roland Warren**
*Good fathers do three things: they provide, they nurture and they guide.*

**Roy Lessin**
*The imprint of a father remains forever on the life of the child.*

**Ruth E. Renkel**
*Sometimes the poorest man leaves his children the richest inheritance.*

**Tony Parsons**
*I have found having my dad as my North Star has worked well for me.*

**Unknown**
*A father is neither an anchor to hold us back nor a sail to take us there, but a guiding light whose love shows us the way.*

**Unknown**
*A dad is someone who wants to catch you when you fall. Instead he picks you up, brushes you off and lets you try again.*

# *Wisdom of Fathers*

### Abraham Lincoln
*No man stands taller than when he stoops to help a child.*

### Barack Obama
*I'm inspired by the love people have for their children. And I'm inspired by my own children, how full they make my heart. They make me want to work to make the world a little bit better. And they make me want to be a better man.*

### Daisy Donovan
*My dad always said, 'Don't worry what people think, because you can't change it.'*

### Daniel Bryan
*I would define the new aspects of fatherhood like this: It is 75% amazing and 25% demoralising. I think any new parent can understand exactly what I'm talking about.*

### Dwayne Wade
*When I say we're learning from our 12-year-old, we're literally learning from our child. So the biggest thing is have an open mind. Go out and research, ask your child, ask other people questions about this, because this conversation is real.*

### David Duchovny
*One of the scary things is that, when you're a kid, you look at your dad as the man who has no fear. When you're an adult, you realize your father had fear, and that you have it, too.*

### David Mitchell
*I've become a less brave traveller since I became a dad, but in the past I was more foolhardy than brave.*

**Dinah Shore**
*The best money advice ever given me was from my father.*
*When I was a little girl, he told me, 'Don't spend anything*
*unless you have to.'*

**Dolly Parton**
*I think I've got my business notions and my sense for that*
*sort of thing from my dad. My dad never had a chance to*
*go to school. He couldn't read and write. But he was so*
*smart. He was just one of those people that could just*
*make the most of anything and everything that he had to*
*work with.*

**Doris Kearns Goodwin**
*Their lifelong love of learning, their remarkable wide-*
*ranging intellectual curiosity, was fostered primarily by*
*their father. He read aloud to them at night, eliciting their*
*responses to works of history and literature. He organized*
*amateur plays for them, encourage pursuit of special*
*interests, prompted them to write essays on their readings,*
*and urge them to recite poetry.*

**Dr. Tony Beizaee**
*Fatherhood is the wisdom to inspire that nothing is*
*impossible to fulfill your children's dream.*

**Eleesha**
*May my children follow their own intuition to discover true*
*empowerment - in the answers they seek.*

*In expression of Fatherhood I evolve to become - all I was*
*destined, to be.*

**Frank Pittman**
*Fathering is not something perfect men do, but something*
*that perfects the man.*

### Harry Truman
*I have found the very best way to advise your children is to find out what they want to do and advise them to do it.*

### Jennie Finch
*And my dad drilled it in my head, you know, 'If you want it bad enough, and you're willing to make the sacrifices, you can do it. But first you have to believe in yourself.*

### Joe Biden
*My dad always said, 'Champ, the measure of a man is not how often he is knocked down, but how quickly he gets up.*

### John Green
*The nature of impending fatherhood is that you are doing something that you're unqualified to do, and then you become qualified while doing it.*

### Josh Charles
*My dad said to me growing up: 'When all is said and done, if you can count all your true friends on one hand, you're a lucky man.'*

### Kevin Hart
*What I've learned as a father is that the most important thing in the world is listening. It's not about trying to be right.*

### Luke Bryan
*From my dad I learned to be good to people, to always be honest and straightforward. I learned hard work and perseverance.*

### Michael Chiklis
*The most challenging part of being a dad is self-restraint. So often your instinct is to teach and tell. I am constantly reminding myself to listen to them.*

### Nadia Scrieva
*It is very easy to be a military strategist, a mercenary, or a king, but much harder to be a father.*

### Nicolas Cage
*Having been a father for 19 years I realise fatherhood has changed me.*

### Pete Wentz
*With marriage and fatherhood, I've finally found two fixed points in my life. They've taught me patience. They've also taught me that I don't need to feel guilty about being happy. My emotional seasons are less extreme.*

### Phil Crane
*As my dad said, you have an obligation to leave the world better than how you found it. And he also reminded us to be givers in this life, and not takers.*

### Phil McGraw
*My dad used to say, 'You wouldn't worry so much about what people thought about you if you knew how seldom they did.'*

### Pink
*My dad raised me with some good advice: 'Always tell the truth. Always shoot from the hip. You might not have many friends, but you'll never have enemies, because people will always know where you're coming from.'*

### Ralph Moody
*Son, there are times a man has to do things he doesn't like to, in order to protect his family.*

*You know, Son, sometimes a fellow has to take a licking for doing the right thing. A licking only lasts a short while, even if it's a hard one, but failing to do the right thing will often make a mark on a man that will last forever.*

*You know, a man's life is a lot like a boat. If he keeps his sail set right it doesn't make too much difference which way the wind blows or which way the current flows. If he knows where he wants to go and keeps his sail trimmed carefully he'll come into the right port. But if he forgets to watch his sail till the current catches him broadside he's pretty apt to smash up on the rocks.*

### Rashida Jones
*My dad always tell me to make decisions from love and not from fear.*

### Rick Riordan
*A father should do more - a father should give more to his children than he takes.*

### Ryan Reynolds
*I don't have to prepare to be wrapped around my daughter's finger. I have been wrapped around her little finger since the day she plopped out into this world.*

### Sigmund Freud
*I cannot think of any need in childhood as strong as the need for a father's protection.*

### Sope Agbelusi
*When my kids tell me "I can't do this dad", I smile and say it's okay. We sit down and we talk about it, I share some of my experiences with them and also let them know it's okay to fail but it is not okay to give before you have tried.*

*One of the primary roles of a parent is to lend your kids some of your confidence enabling them to get their own.*

### Tim Allen
*Dad needs to show an incredible amount of respect and humor and friendship toward his mate so the kids understand their parents are sexy, they're fun, they do things together, they're best friends. Kids learn by example. If I respect Mom, they're going to respect Mom.*

### Tim Russert
*The older I get, the smarter my father seems to get.*

### Tim Wolfe
*[Man adopts] a role called Being a Father so that his child would have something mythical and infinitely important: a Protector, who would keep a lid on all the chaotic and catastrophic possibilities of life.*

### Tom Hanks
*I will do anything I can possibly do in order to keep you safe. That's it. Offer that up and then just love them.*

### Umberto Eco
*I believe that what we become depends on what our fathers teach us at odd moments, when they aren't trying to teach us. We are formed by little scraps of wisdom.*

### William Shakespeare
*It is a wise father that knows his own child.*

# Quotes about Daughters

**Adriana Trigiani**
*He gives her the best gift a woman can get in this world: protection. And the little girl learns to trust the man in her life.*

**Agatha Stephanie Lin**
*Daddy, thanks for being my hero, chauffeur, financial support, listener, life mentor, friend, guardian and simply being there every time I need a hug.*

**Alison Lohman**
*There will always be a few people who have the courage to love what is untamed inside us. One of those men is my father.*

**Ama H. Vanniarachchy**
*A father's tears and fears are unseen, his love is unexpressed, but his care and protection remain as a pillar of strength throughout our lives.*

**Arab Proverb**
*No one is able to make the female a queen except her father.*

**Bindi Irwin**
*My Daddy was my hero. He was always there for me when I needed him. He listened to me and taught me so many things. But most of all he was fun.*

**Chance The Rapper**
*My best smile is probably when I'm holding my daughter.*

### Christopher Hitchens
*To be the father of growing daughters is to understand something of what Yeats evokes with his imperishable phrase 'terrible beauty.' Nothing can make one so happily exhilarated or so frightened: it's a solid lesson in the limitations of self to realize that your heart is running around inside someone else's body. It also makes me quite astonishingly calm at the thought of death: I know whom I would die to protect and I also understand that nobody but a lugubrious serf can possibly wish for a father who never goes away.*

### David Duchovny
*The happiest moment of my life was probably when my daughter was born.*

### Dawn French
*It was my father who taught me to value myself. He told me that I was uncommonly beautiful and that I was the most precious thing in his life.*

### Dusty Baker
*I love my daughter, but she had me on couscous and fixed me pastas and made me eat oatmeal every morning and what else, turkey burgers, turkey bacon, and that kind of stuff. So she wants her dad to live a long time, and I do, too.*

### Dr. James Dobson
*A good father will leave his imprint on his daughter for the rest of her life.*

### Dumitru D. Coman
*My life is a fairy tale because it revolves around a princess —my beautiful daughter.*

**Elaine S. Dalton**
*The greatest thing a father can do for his daughter is to love her mother.*

*The greatest thing a father can do for his daughter is to love her mother.*

**Elton John**
*It was a reminder that you only get so long, that you never know what's around the corner. Maybe that gave me some real clarity about what was important to me about life. Why try and deny how you really feel, deep down, about something as fundamental as fatherhood?*

**Emily Henry**
*What I didn't know to expect is that today, I would feel like I'd been born too. You have made a new person: January's father. And I know this is who I will be for the rest of my life.*

**Emily Mortimer**
*I want any excuse to come home. My dad is not a spring chicken any more. If anyone says, 'Go buy a postage stamp in London,' I'll go and do it.*

**Emily VanCamp**
*I think women look for that quality in a man of being a good dad whether they're immediately wanting to be a parent or not.*

**Emily Mortimer**
*My dad had this philosophy that if you tell children they're beautiful and wonderful then they believe it, and they will be. So I never thought I was unattractive. But I was never one of the girls at school who had lots of boyfriends.*

**Euripides**
*To a father growing old, nothing is dearer than a daughter.*

**Fanny Fern**
*To her, the name of father was another name for love.*

**Garrison Keillor**
*The father of a daughter is nothing but a high-class hostage.  A father turns a stony face to his sons, berates them, shakes his antlers, paws the ground, snorts, runs them off into the underbrush, but when his daughter puts her arm over his shoulder and says, 'Daddy, I need to ask you something,' he is a pat of butter in a hot frying pan.*

**Gloria Naylor**
*Old as she was, she still missed her daddy sometimes.*

**Greg Louganis**
*Mom was the one who taught me unconditional love. With Dad, I'd always felt there was something to live up to - expectations. But in the last year, we had a wonderful relationship.*

**Gregory E. Lang**
*A daughter needs a dad to be the standard against she will judge all men.*

**Guy Lombardo**
*Many a man wishes he were strong enough to tear a telephone book in half—especially if he has a teenage daughter.*

**Guy Ritchie**
*I love fatherhood. I could bang on about kids forever.*

**Gwyneth Paltrow**
*My father, he was like the rock, the guy you went to with every problem.*

### Hall Caine
*He was all iron outside, but all father within.*

### Halle Berry
*I know that I will never find my father in any other man who comes into my life, because it is a void in my life that can only be filled by him.*

### Harper Lee
*She did not stand alone, but what stood behind her, the most potent moral force in her life, was the love of her father.*

### Harry Connick, Jr.
*I think a dad has to make his daughter feel that he's genuinely interested in what she's going through.*

### Hedy Lamarr
*I am not ashamed to say that no man I ever met was my father's equal, and I never loved any other man as much.*

### Hendrith Vanlon Smith Jr.
*Daughters always revel in their mother's admiration. And daughters always bask in their father's love.*

*Daughters need their dads. And only a dad can be a dad*

*Fatherhood is important to me. I've taught my daughter to cherish nature, to nurture her spirituality, to love herself, to love others, to exploration science, and to seek wisdom and understanding. I make it a point to cultivate those things in her, in the way that only a father can.*

*I'm so grateful — the love me and my daughter Chaya share is so powerful and so potent and so pure. What we give each other is unconditional and unrestrained love. We pour that love into each other, and we embrace that love from each other with thankful hearts. So much so, that parts of ourselves live within the other. Nothing and no one could separate us. Nothing and no one could jeopardize our love. That's the magnitude of our daddy daughter love. That's me and Chaya.*

### Honoré de Balzac
*I, and I only, am to blame for all their sins; I spoiled them. To-day they are as eager for pleasure as they used to be for sugar-plums. When they were little girls I indulged them in every whim. They had a carriage of their own when they were fifteen. They have never been crossed. I am guilty, and not they—but I sinned through love.*

### Hugh Jackman
*When I come home, my daughter will run to the door and give me a big hug, and everything that's happened that day just melts away.*

### Idris Elba
*I watch my daughter wanting to be like other kids and getting upset that she's not.  But I always try and instill in her the idea that she's perfect as she is.*

### J. Richard Singleton
*No man wants his daughter to be the kind of girl whom he liked in high school.*

### Jake Owen
*I look at my little girl and I wonder what she's going to be and what she's going to do and what is it that leads girls certain directions in life. I think a lot of that goes back to what kind of father they had, and so it makes me want to be the best dad I can possibly be.*

**James Earl Jones**
*More and more, when I single out the person out who inspired me most, I go back to my grandfather.*

**James T. Adams**
*Any astronomer can predict with absolute accuracy just where every star in the universe will be at 11:30 tonight. He can make no such prediction about his teenage daughter.*

**Jason Reynolds**
*Again, dove into each other. This time the hug, a mix of I miss you and who are you and I'm confused and I'm cracking and I don't know what the hell to do or where the hell to go. My father's hand gripped my back as I did my best to bury myself in his armpit, to get lost in the new and strangely familiar feeling of fatherhood.*

**Jim Bishop**
*Watching your daughter being collected by her date feels like handing over a million-dollar Stradivarius to a gorilla.*

**Jim DeMint**
*One of the greatest titles in the world is parent, and one of the biggest blessings in the world is to have parents to call mom and dad.*

**Joe Rigney**
*My one-year-old walks up to me with arms outstretched. I can see it in his eyes. He is searching for something: approval, affirmation, acceptance. The kind that only a father can give. He is hungry for a father's love, for the Father's love. Either the laughter in my eyes, the smile on my face, and the strength and tenderness of my arms will tell the truth about God, or their absence will blaspheme the Father of lights. My son is reaching for me, and looking for God. My son, the theologian.*

### Jimmy Fallon
*Dads immediately fall in love with their little girls and will let them get away with everything. So, moms are going to have to be the disciplinarians when it comes to daughters.*

### John A. Passaro
*Today is not the real Father's Day. It is the man made version. The real Father's Day are the other 364 other days of the year that I get to see my boys grow into men and my girls grow into ladies and feel I had a slight part of the people that they turned out to be. Not a better feeling in the world. With every life lesson taught, half of which are understood at the time, and the other half that are understood after I am told to stop being ridiculous - EVERYDAY is Father's Day. And I wouldn't trade it for the world. Good and bad. I can honestly say there is no feeling on earth, like being a father and a dad.*

### John Birmingham
*When a parent dies, for those left behind it can feel as though half the sky has fallen. My father was the sheltering sky, and beneath his mild firmament no storm ever raged, no hard rain fell.*

### John Denver
*At times I've got a really big ego. But I'll tell you the best thing about me. I'm some guy's dad I'm some little gal's dad. When I die, if they say I was Annie's husband and Zachary John and Anna Kate's father, boy, that's enough for me to be remembered by. That's more than enough.*

### John Leguizamo
*Every dad who loves his daughter is not going to want her to go with the penniless slacker loser poet bum, when she could go out with someone who's successful.*

### John Mayer
*Fathers, be good to your daughters. You are the god and the weight of her world.*

### John Sinor
*It is admirable for a man to take his son fishing, but there is a special place in heaven for the father who takes his daughter shopping.*

### Johnny Vegas
*You always hear people saying, 'I hope I'm not turning into my dad', but I'd be honoured if I became half as decent a bloke as he is.*

### Joseph Addison
*Certain is it that there is no kind of affection so purely angelic as of a father to a daughter.*

### Josh Hatcher
*So, you're handed a baby and a new name (Daddy) and you now have to choose to accept the challenge. Here's the thing. I don't believe that rejecting it's an option. I mean, people DO reject it. But you shouldn't. You choose then and there to be a father. And you make that choice, day in and day out to make sure their needs are met, that the example is set for them, that they are loved, cherished, corrected, and challenged. You have to choose it.*

### Kazuo Koike
*A father knows his child's heart, as only a child can know his fathers.*

### Kevin Hart
*I took my daughter to the father-daughter dance, and I cried like a little baby. She's 11 years old, so seeing her get dressed up and pretty made me cry.*

### Kristan Higgins
*There should be some drug for fathers of teenage girls. Something that calmed your heart so it didn't practically rip through your chest. Something that could soothe the fury your daughter could inspire, the absolute terror that something unspeakable would happen to her, the almost murderous sense of protection. Something that would give you the words to tell her that no one would ever love her as much as dear old dad, and if she just listened to him, she'd have a much easier time of things and be safe from boys who ruined her life.*

### Lady Gaga
*I love my Daddy. My Daddy's everything. I hope I can find a man that will treat me as good as my dad.*

### Laura Gentile
*He would not live the life of his daughter by falling apart and not giving her anything but anticipated grief and collateral heartache. He wanted to imprint paternal love on her body. Maybe she would be strong and regenerated enough to stay, and maybe his intense affection would work its magic.*

### Linda Poindexter
*When my father didn't have my hand, he had my back.*

**Liza Minelli**
*My mother gave me my drive, but my father gave me my dreams.*

**Lydia Maria Child**
*No music is so pleasant to my ears as that word—father.*

**Lydia Netzer**
*A child playing with its father screams louder, laughs harder, jumps more eagerly, puts more faith in everything.*

**Mandi Hart**
*I think it's much easier for a man to have children than for children to have a father. Children need their fathers more than we think. A father spurs a child on to succeed. A fathers love gives his children wings and confidence in life.*

**Mark Maish**
*Every child grows up thinking their father is a hero or villain until they are old enough to realize that he is just a man.*

**Martin Sheen**
*We never get over our fathers, and we're not required to.*

**Matt Haig**
*I loved her, instantly. Of course, most parents love their children instantly. But I mention it here because I still find it a remarkable thing. Where was that love before? Where did you acquire it from? The way it is suddenly there, total and complete, as sudden as grief, but in reverse, is one of the wonders about being human.*

### Matthew McConaughey
*The only thing I ever knew I wanted to be was a father. To me, fatherhood meant a man had made it in life. Growing up, I said "yes sir" and "no sir" to my father and his friends because they were fathers. Fatherhood, what I most revered in life, what I was most impressed with, was now what I was about to become more involved with. The message of manhood that came to me at my own father's passing had newborn relevance as I became one myself. Yes sir.*

### Marinela Reka
*Being a daddy's girl is like having a permanent armor for the rest of your life.*

### Marisol Santiago
*A girl's first true love is her father.*

### Marlin S. Potash
*A good father loves his daughter with no strings attached. He is available. He is both strong and tender. Being big and strong doesn't mean being separate from one's feelings; to the contrary, it means being very much in touch with them. Women who experienced fathers like that know that a strong man can cry, and that a man who can cry can also be very strong.*

### Mat Johnson
*A man's daughter is his heart. Just with feet, walking out in the world.*

### Melanie White
*You gotta love dads. At my wedding, when I tripped on my wedding dress and fell flat on my face, Dad said, 'Don't worry, you'll do better next time.*

### Michael Josephson
*One of the greatest things about daughters is how they adored you when they were little; how they rushed into your arms with electric delight and demanded that you watch everything they do and listen to everything they say.*

### Michael Ratnadeepak
*No one in this world can love a girl more than her father.*

### Miley Cyrus
*I've got high standards when it comes to boys. As my dad says, all girls should! I'm from the South - Tennessee, to be exact - and down there, we're all about southern hospitality. I know that if I like a guy, he better be nice, and above all, my dad has to approve of him!*

### Miranda Lambert
*I've dated all kinds of guys and didn't know who I'd end up with. But I kind of assumed it would be someone more like my dad than not.*

### Mitch Albom
*If you want the experience of having complete responsibility for another human being, and to learn how to love and bond in the deepest way, then you should have children.*

### Natasha Josefowitz
*My father died many years ago, and yet when something special happens to me, I talk to him secretly not really knowing whether he hears, but it makes me feel better to half believe it.*

### Nina George
*...having a child is like casting off your own childhood forever. It's as if it's only then that you really grasp what it means to be a man. You're scared too that all your weaknesses will be laid bare, because fatherhood demands more than you can give.... I always felt I had to earn your love, because I loved you so, so much.*

**Nitya Prakash**
*Confident women are raised by loving dads.*

**Orson Scott Card**
*I hope I am remembered by my children as a good father.*

**Philippa Gregory**
*I can speak of our baby like this to no one else. Who but his father would linger over the exact width of his gummy little smile or the blueness of his eyes, or the sweetness of his little lick of tawny hair on his forehead?*

**Randy Harrison**
*Dad said that he was prouder of me than he'd ever been when I came out.*

**Richelle E. Goodrich**
*A father's success does not depend upon his ability to work and provide, to guard and protect, or to lecture and discipline. A father's success does not depend upon his ability to guide and govern, to instruct and demonstrate, or to remedy and repair. A father's success does not depend upon his ability to understand and relate, to adapt and change, or to entertain and play. A father's success does, however, greatly depend upon his ability to love and be loved.*

**Richard L. Ratliff**
*Fathers and daughters have a special bond.  She is always daddy's little girl.*

**Robert Carlyle**
*I've always taken my love of children from my father. He was a children magnet. Suddenly, having my first child hit home what my dad went through.*

### Ryan Reynolds
*I don't have to prepare to be wrapped around my daughter's finger. I have been wrapped around her little finger since the day she plopped out into this world.*

### Sachin Ramdas Bharatiya
*For father, his daughter is no less than a breath.*

### Sage Steadman
*He was not being courageous as he bore the freezing stream for his wife and children. He simply chose between the lesser of two evils—the pain and suffering he would endure in the river, a physical pain that he could stand to bear, or the pain and suffering he would feel if he had to watch his family wade across and freeze. It was not a decision. The choice had already been made the moment Ole proposed marriage to his wife and welcomed these beautiful daughters into the world.*

### Samuel L. Jackson
*My dad was an absentee dad, so it was always important to me that I was part of my daughter's life...*

### Sammy Davis, Jr.
*I wasn't anything special as a father. But I loved them and they knew it.*

### Sarah Morgan
*This is embarrassing." Hannah sniffed. "I'm too old to be crying on your shoulder." "You're never too old to cry on your dad's shoulder, although I have to admit I hate to see you cry."*

### Sarah Orne Jewett
*My dear father; my dear friend; the best and wisest man I ever knew, who taught me many lessons and showed me many things as we went together along the country by-ways.*

### Scott Spencer
*He welcomes the chance to do fatherly things with the little girl, and those ten morning minutes with dear little four-year-old Ruby, with her deep soulful eyes, and the wondrous things she sees with them, and her deep soulful voice, and the precious though not entirely memorable things she says with it, and the smell of baby shampoo and breakfast cereal filling the car, that little shimmering capsule of time is like listening to cello music in the morning, or watching birds in a flutter of industry building a nest, it simply reminds you that even if God is dead, or never existed in the first place, there is, nevertheless, something tender at the center of creation, some meaning, some purpose and poetry.*

### Sean Norris
*Some boys grow up to be great men, some grow up to be great fathers, and while most grow up to be neither, none grow up to be both.*

### Sean Thompson
*Fatherhood  is my religion.*

### Stanley Behrman
*When my daughter says, 'Daddy, I need you!' I wonder if she has any idea that I need her billion times more.*

### Stanley T. Banks
*You fathers will understand. You have a little girl. She looks up to you. You're her oracle. You're her hero. And then the day comes when she gets her first permanent wave and goes to her first real party, and from that day on, you're in a constant state of panic.*

### Stella Payton

*Beautiful is the man who leaves a legacy that of shared love and life. It is he who transfers meaning, assigns significance and conveys in his loving touch the fine art and gentle shaping of a life. This man shall be called, Father.*

### Stephen Colbert

*My daughter said, 'Why are you yelling at us?' and I said, 'I'm trying to discipline you!' And then she looked up at me with her tear-stained eyes and said, 'This is how you teach children, by making them cry.' And it was such a clenching reminder — she won not only the argument, but she won life with that statement. I just burst out laughing, and I think they were so surprised that I burst out laughing, that they did too.*

### Susan Gale

*A father's smile has been known to light up a child's entire day.*

### Taylor Swift

*My dad believed in me, even when I didn't. He always knew I could do this.*

### Terri Guillemets

*I love my father as the stars—he's a bright shining example and a happy twinkling in my heart.*

### Tracy Morgan

*Having a daughter makes you see things in a different way. This is my only girl. So, I don't care what it takes to protect her. You can call it what you want to call it. As long as you treat her the same way I treat her, like my princess, I don't mind.*

***Unknown***

*A father is a son's first hero and a daughter's first love.*

∽    ∾

*I may find my prince, but my dad will always be my king.*

∽    ∾

*A father's job is not to teach his daughter how to be a lady. It's to teach her how a lady should be treated.*

∽    ∾

*A father holds his daughter's hand for a short while, but he holds her heart forever.*

∽    ∾

*A little girl giggles when she is denied an ice cream by her mother. She knows daddy will get her some later.*

∽    ∾

*The most admirable thing ever has to be a father protecting his daughter.*

∽    ∾

*One of life's greatest mysteries is how the boy who wasn't good enough to marry your daughter can be the father of the smartest grandchild in the world.*

∽    ∾

*Behind every great daughter is a truly amazing father.*

### Vincent Carrella
*A father is only capable of giving what he has, and what he knows. A good father gives all of himself that is good.*

### Wade Boggs
*Anyone can be a father, but it takes someone special to be a dad, and that's why I call you dad, because you are so special to me.*

### Warren Farrell
*Fatherhood was about your dad trading in the old glint in his*

# *Fatherhood Quotes about Sons*

**Aldous Huxley**
*Sons have always a rebellious wish to be disillusioned by that which charmed their fathers.*

**Bill Gray**
*Good dads forgive your mistakes. Great dads help you hide them from mom.*

**Billy Graham**
*The greatest tribute a boy can give to his father is to say, 'When I grow up, I want to be just like my dad.'*

**Boomer Esiason**
*My goal is for Gunnar to outlive me. That's the way it should be. My dream is for him to be a dad himself one day, so he can find out all the anxiety that kids bring to their dads.*

**Brick Stone**
*New dads aren't aware that infants are both blessings and black holes that drain sleep, time, and passion.*

**Charles Kettering**
*Every father should remember one day his son will follow his example, not his advice.*

**Charles Wadworth**
*By the time a man realizes that maybe his father was right, he usually has a son who thinks he's wrong.*

**Chris Martin**
*Men should always change diapers. It's mentally cleansing. It's like washing dishes, but imagine if the dishes were your kids, so you really love the dishes.*

**Clayton Lessor**
*When a boy feels as if no one cares about him, or as if he will never amount to anything, he truly believes it doesn't matter what he does.*

ஒ  ௸

*There's a wound most troubled boys share, which, at its core, comes from the feeling that they don't have their father's unconditional love.*

**Daniel Baldwin**
*My little son, Atticus, desperately needs his dad and I haven't been there for him... and that's sad.*

**Donald Miller**
*I know, from the three visits I made to him, the blended composite of love and fear that exists only in a boy's notion of his father.*

**Emily Mortimer**
*My dad had this philosophy that if you tell children they're beautiful and wonderful then they believe it, and they will be. So I never thought I was unattractive. But I was never one of the girls at school who had lots of boyfriends.*

**Enid Bagnold**
*A father is always making his baby into a little woman. And when she is a woman, he turns her back again.*

**Fathima Arshard**
*I know a man whose arms carried me high on days that I felt low. A man whose arms I'll never outgrow.*

**Frank A. Clark**
*A father is a man who expects his son to be as good a man as he meant to be.*

### Fredrik Backman
*Sons want their fathers' attention until the precise moment when fathers want their sons'.*

### George Best
*The best thing about being a dad? Well, I think it's just the thing that every man wants - to have a son and heir.*

### Hendrith Vanlon Smith, Jr.
*Sons always revel in their fathers admiration. Sons always bask in their mother's love.*

### Herbert Kaufman
*Rich men's sons are seldom rich men's fathers.*

### Ian Morgan Cron
*A boy needs a father to show him how to be in the world. He needs to be given swagger, taught how to read a map so that he can recognize the roads that lead to life and the paths that lead to death, how to know what love requires, and where to find steel in the heart when life makes demands on us that are greater than we think we can endure.*

### Isaac Mogilevsky
*Fathers have a way of either distorting the character of God or rightly representing it to their son.*

### James A. Baldwin
*If the relationship of father to son could really be reduced to biology, the whole earth would blaze with the glory of fathers and sons.*

### James Caan
*I never saw my dad cry. My son saw me cry. My dad never told me he loved me, and consequently I told Scott I loved*

*him every other minute. The point is, I'll make less mistakes than my dad, my sons hopefully will make less mistakes than me, and their sons will make less mistakes than their dads.*

### Jamie Redknapp
*I know I'm 25 now, but there's still that little lad inside me who likes his dad there to see him.*

### Janvier Chouteu-Chando
*Nothing crushes the soul of a father more than the loss of the beloved son he failed to lavish his love on.*

### Jason Versey
*Our sons not only receive a name but a legacy. With keen eyes they watch and learn. At their core, they are shaped by the very things we say and don't say; and by what we do and don't do. They may cling to what is noble, they may emulate our flaws or reject them all together but a legacy will be formed nonetheless. It's a huge undertaking but one I know the Lord will see me through.*

### John Steinbeck
*Why do men like me want sons?" he wondered. "It must be because they hope in their poor beaten souls that these new men, who are their blood, will do the things they were not strong enough nor wise enough nor brave enough to do. It is rather like another chance at life; like a new bag of coins at a table of luck after your fortune is gone.*

### Kevin Alan Milne
*...it was never the sun overhead that brightened my days. It was the son playing on my lap.*

**Matthew Buckley**
*Being a father means you have to think fast on your feet. You must be judicious, wise, brave, tender, and willing to put on a frilly hat and sit down to a pretend tea party.*

**Mekael Shane**
*Sons are born to make their fathers better men.*

**Michael Ratnadeepak**
*No one in this world can love a girl more than her father.*

**Nick Harkaway**
*I can show him how to be the right kind of stupid.*

**Randy Alcorn**
*It's my responsibility to cultivate the man in my son. I can't be passive about that.*

*Father to teenage son: "My relationship with you is more important than anything I've got to say to you."*

**Ray Romano**
*Having children is like living in a frat house. Nobody sleeps, everything's broken, and there's a lot of throwing up.*

**Reed Markham**
*Being a great father is like shaving. No matter how good you shaved today, you have to do it again tomorrow.*

**Richard Ford**
*He needed me to do what sons do for their fathers: bear witness that they're substantial, that they're not hollow, not ringing absences. That they count for something when little else seems to.*

### Rob Kozak
*I am a proud father in the accomplishments of my son, who fills my heart with joy and my mind with favourable wonderings. He enhances my purpose on this wondrous planet. Parents, be aware that not only are you a model for your children, but in some fashions they are models for you — taking life easy, with a spirit of adventure. Encourage your kids to be kids!*

### Russell Westbrook
*I think fatherhood would change anybody when you have your first son. It's been amazing.*

### Steve Martin
*A father carries pictures where his money used to be.*

### Terri Guillemets
*Every son quotes his father, in words and in deeds.*

### The Talmud
*When you teach your son, you teach your son's son.*

### Unknown
*When I first time held my son in my hands, I had a feeling like I am Superman. One day when he's grown up, he will realise his father is just a regular guy who wears a cap, but a real life Superman for him.*

### Unknown
*I pledge to become a great father to my new born kid. For me he's everything from now onwards.*

*Becoming father of a little angel gives me immense pleasure and happiness. She's my precious and I am her saviour.*

*Every man a woman meets is measured through her father's eyes.*

೬⌒ ⌒೨

*I am happy to become father of a cute boy, as he will soon be my playstation partner. Lot's of action and adventure for me and the baby coming in near future.*

೬⌒ ⌒೨

*Great men are not born, but moulded by their fathers and their fathers before them.*

### Walter M. Schirra
*You don't raise heroes, you raise sons. And if you treat them like sons, they'll turn out to be heroes, even if it's just in your own eyes.*

### Wayne Rooney
*Becoming a dad means you have to be a role model for your son and be someone he can look up to.*

### William Shakespeare
*When a father gives to his son, both laugh; when a son gives to his father, both cry.*

# *Fathers as Heroes*

**Alex Pettyfer**
*My dad's one of my biggest heroes. I also think Paul Newman's an inspiration. I know a lot of people say that, but I love that he's a great role model and a humanitarian. I admire people who don't necessarily want to change the world, but try to make it a better environment.*

**Andre Dubus III**
*One of the accidental joys of my writing life has been that I've had some lovely, surprisingly good fortune with readers, and I've brought readers to my dad's work. I can't tell you the joy that gives me. Because my father's work was masterful.*

**Caitlyn Jenner**
*If I were to compare the Olympic decathlon to fatherhood, I would say fatherhood is a lot tougher.*

**David Alan Grier**
*When I was a kid, I wanted to walk with my dad's limp - my dad was my hero - but that infuriated him, and he would make me walk back and forth in the living room until I walked without it.*

**David Boreanaz**
*Growing up, I saw my dad do charity work for children with health issues. That had a profound effect on me.*

**David Rudisha**
*I realised I could run after finding out that my dad used to run and it gave me the morale that if he did it then maybe I could also run.*

**Dean Norris**
*My dad's era believed that there was something noble in being a good guy - the kind of guy that lived straight and narrow, told the truth, and stood up for what he believed was right.*

**Erika Cosby**
*Fathers just have a way of putting everything together.*

**Habeeb Akande**
*Behind every great man is a man greater, his father.*

**Harry Connick, Jr.**
*My Dad is my hero.*

**John L. Phillips**
*My dad served in two wars has been flying airplanes for 60 years now. He was certainly quite an inspiration.*

**Johnny Vegas**
*I came back from university thinking I knew all about politics and racism, not knowing my dad had been one of the youngest-serving Labour councillors in the town and had refused to work in South Africa years ago because of the situation there. And he's never mentioned it - you just find out. That's a real man to me. A sleeping lion.*

**Kate Baer**
*What kind of man does not give up his time, his many pleasures, but hands them over without a sound. What kind of man bends to hold them in their suffering, in their questions, in their garbled turns of phrase. What kind of man admits his failures, turns over his heavy stones, stands at the feet of grief and wanting does not turn away. What kind of man becomes a father. A lasting place. A steady ship inside a tireless storm.*

**Leona Lewis**
*My dad is such a good man. You know how when you are a child you think your dad is invincible? Well, I still think that - he is so wise and everything I do I ask my dad's advice about first.*

**Michael Bassey Johnson**
*Fathers are the pillars of the home. Without them, the citadel of confidence crumbles. Without them, the tendrils of hope withers. Without them, sweet and great dreams turn to nightmares.*

**Pam Brown**
*Dads are most ordinary men turned by love into heroes, adventures, story-tellers, and singers of songs.*

**Patrick Swayze**
*I like to believe that I've got a lot of guardian warriors sittin' on my shoulder including my dad.*

**Seann William Scott**
*My role model is my dad.*

**Unknown**
*Dad: A son's first hero, a daughter's first love.*

# *Fathers as Friends – Support*

### Adam Sandler
*I mean, I look at my dad. He was twenty when he started having a family, and he was always the coolest dad. He did everything for his kids, and he never made us feel like he was pressured. I know that it must be a great feeling to be a guy like that.*

### Amy Sedaris
*David and Dad didn't get along too well growing up. I mean we all got along, but it was harder on David, because David wasn't going to be the son that Dad wanted. But now they're like best friends.*

### Candace Parker
*On my best days, such as when I was a junior in high school coming off a 42-point performance and near triple-double, my dad was there to tell me I haven't arrived yet and bring me back to reality.*

### Caroline Wozniacki
*My dad has always been my coach. And I've spent so much time with him. So he's one of my best friends. And I can talk to him about everything.*

### Drake
*Me and my dad are friends. We're cool. I'll never be disappointed again, because I don't expect anything anymore from him. I just let him exist, and that's how we get along.*

### Émile Gaboriau

*A father is the one friend upon whom we can always rely. In the hour of need, when all else fails, we remember him upon whose knees we sat when children, and who soothed our sorrows; and even though he may be unable to assist us, his mere presence serves to comfort and strengthen us.*

### Gwyneth Paltrow

*My father, he was like the rock, the guy you went to with every problem.*

### Jack Osbourne

*If I have a problem, stuff's going through my head, I feel like using, I usually go and talk to my dad...*

### John Wooden

*I was built up from my dad more than anyone else.*

### Josh Hatcher

*Your kids need you to be present - but that doesn't mean in the building, playing X-Box and yelling at them. Change diapers. Show them how to treat their mother by treating her good yourself. Tell them that you love them. Laugh with them.*

### Kim Wilde

*Dad is my best mate and I can tell Mum absolutely anything. I really appreciate Mum and Dad. Why are we so close? Young parents, I think. The rock business keeps their minds young.*
*When my father didn't have my hand, he had my back.*

### Peter Mullan

*As a dad I'm emotionally dedicated but I'm not 'figuring out their life plans'. But of course as I'm telling them about the rights of wrongs I'm thinking back to what I was like at their age.*

### Richelle E. Goodrich
*The greatest lessons I learned from my father didn't come from lectures or discipline or even time spent together. What has stuck with me is his example. From watching, I chose whether to be or not to be like him.*

### Tiger Woods
*My dad was my best friend and greatest role model. He was an amazing dad, coach, mentor, soldier, husband and friend.*

### Tracy Morgan
*I deal with my sons like young men. If they have a problem with something, they come to me. I am the type of dad that will drop everything I am doing for them, and always tell them to talk to me about it.*

# *Bittersweet*

### Anaïs Nin
*I stopped loving my father a long time ago. What remained was the slavery to a pattern.*

### Bear Grylls
*I loved climbing because of the freedom, and having time and space. I remember coming off Everest for the last time, thinking of Dad and wishing that he could have seen what I saw. He would have loved it.*

### Bubba Watson
*My dad's not here, but he's watching in heaven.*

### Charley Pride
*I grew up not liking my father very much. I never saw him cry. But he must have. Everybody cries.*

### Chief Joseph
*I pressed my father's hand and told him I would protect his grave with my life. My father smiled and passed away to the spirit land.*

### Conrad Hall
*Dad, wherever you are, you are gone but you will never be forgotten.*

### Courtney Love
*I like all the angels around because they protect me and my daughter. I mean, her Dad's an angel.*

### Dean Koontz
*There's sometimes a weird benefit to having an alcoholic, violent father. He really motivated me in that I never wanted to be anything like him.*

**E. B. White**
*The time not to become a father is eighteen years before a war.*

**Eddie Murray**
*No one was more important than my mom and dad. I know they are watching from a place up in heaven here today to make sure all their kids are doing good.*

**Eric Shanteau**
*Obviously, losing a parent is very difficult. I miss my dad every day, but I know he would be proud to see me continuing to swim and going for another shot at the Olympics.*

**Geoffrey Hill**
*Finally coming to terms with Fathers Day. I blow as a Dad. I get it. No, I'm not an evil, abusive Father, it's just that while all my intentions and thoughts have been out of love for my kids, my actions and behaviour never measured up.*

**Hanya Yanagihara**
*I thought those thoughts all men think when a woman tells them she's pregnant: What would the baby look like? Would I like it? Would I love it? And then, more crushingly: fatherhood. With all its responsibilities and fulfillments and tedium and possibilities for failure.*

**Horace**
*Undeservedly you will atone for the sins of your fathers.*

**Jack Kerouac**
*It's terrible never to find a father in a world chock-full of fathers of all sorts.*

**Jean de La Fontaine**
*It is impossible to please all the world and one's father.*

### Joey Lauren Adams
*My life isn't that dramatic. My dad really loves me, he just can't talk on the phone. He's too crippled and shy, and that's almost harder. He's there and he loves me, and I try and try and try, it's just impossible to have a relationship.*

### John Ciardi
*Every parent is at some time the father of the unreturned prodigal, with nothing to do but keep his house open to hope.*

### Lenny Kravitz
*A dramatic thing, the first time you stand up to your dad.*

### Michael Bergin
*A father's disappointment can be a very powerful tool.*

### Mitch Albom
*My dad barely moved. He never asked what happened. But to this day, I can still feel his waist in my wet grip, and the comfort it gave me. For many years, that was my perception of fatherhood, a place where a child can find sanctuary. Perhaps this is why I took over the orphanage. Perhaps I've grown into my father that way.*

### P.S. Jagadeesh Kumar
*A father's love is like your shadow, though he is dead or alive, he will live with your shadow.*

# The Responsibility of Fathers

### Chad Judice
*Any man has the capability of making a baby, but the responsibility of fatherhood is a gift bestowed upon those wise enough to realize that it is a lifelong commitment that will bring one a joy no amount of money on this earth can buy. One cannot fully understand the unconditional love of Jesus Christ until they can love something greater than themselves. There is no better teacher of this lesson than fatherhood.*

### Chris O'Donnell
*I think it's easiest to teach by example. My dad didn't tell us to work hard we just saw how hard he worked. I know I have shortcomings - like a short fuse - but I've learned you can't come home from a long day of work and snap at the kids.*

### Chris Robinson
*Life is different than it was in the Nineties. I'm a dad, and there are other things I have to get done in an afternoon than just being an artist.*

### Clayton Lessor
*Teaching a boy to be a man is the primary job of a father.*

### Colin Hanks
*My dad has always been extremely supportive in every decision I've made and much more interested in me picking what I wanted to do.*

### Corey Hart
*I needed to step away from music because the truth was I couldn't be the dad I wanted to be to my kids. My truth was that I could not reconcile the two worlds - the entertainment world and being the dad I wanted to be in the present. You can't substitute time, you just can't.*

**Craig D. Lounsbrough**
*To lead solely on the behalf of those being led is the utter pinnacle of fatherhood, and it is sad that so few ever stand on the summit.*

ھى ھى

*A father is the man who realizes that a life spent in the service of his children is the creation of a legacy so vast that it can be deeply drawn from for generations to come, but it will never be emptied by any who come to it.*

ھى ھى

*A father is the man who can change a world he will not be part of by building the tiny human that is part of him.*

**Craig Wilkinson**
*It is no exaggeration to say that fatherlessness is the most harmful demographic trend of this generation. It is the engine driving our most urgent social problems". I am convinced that the damage to humanity caused by the epidemic of unfathered men and women is far greater than the damage caused by war and disease combined.*

**Dan Pearce**
*The greatest mark of a father is how he treats his children when no one is looking.*

**Derek Prince**
*In a certain sense God has committed to every father the responsibility to embody, as a person, the ultimate revelation of the Bible, fatherhood. To be a real father is the most perfect depiction of God that any man can achieve, because it is the ultimate revelation of God Himself. In fact, every father represents God to his family. That is not an option! The question is, Do you as a father represent God rightly or wrongly?*

### Diane Lane
*I was raised by free-spirited people, though my father gave me a very strong work ethic.*

### Dionne Warwick
*Do you know that other than my father, I've never had a man take care of me?*

### Donald DeMarco
*The absence of fatherhood implies the impossibility of brotherhood. It is no accident that Schopenhauer, Nietzsche, and Sartre, in addition to Freud, all struggled with the notion of fatherlessness. Its exalted, but unrealistic, implication is godlessness and self-deification. But its more immediate, existential implication, as we have seen, is being orphaned and abandoned. It is curious that Freud, despite his extensive knowledge of classic literature, either ignored or repressed its most trenchant moral, namely, that by equating oneself with the gods, one invokes their anger and punishment. The gods will not be mocked, and they are intolerant of hubris.*

### Edward O. Sisson
*The secret of the whole matter is that a habit is not the mere tendency to repeat a certain act, nor is it established by the mere repetition of the act. Habit is a fixed tendency to react or respond in a certain way to a given stimulus; and the formation of habit always involves the two elements, the stimulus and the response or reaction. The indolent lad goes to school not in response to any stimulus in the school itself, but to the pressure of his father's will; when that stimulus is absent, the reaction as a matter of course does not occur.*

### Elizabeth Lesser
*Full-hearted fatherhood might save the world.*

### Ephantus Mwenda Njagi
*True men embrace their responsibility. They know being a father should be real, not just owning a name.*

### Fahad Basheer
*Father is an animal the moment he loves his public reputation more than his children but a father becomes the father of his children, the moment he loves his children more than his public reputation. Fathers who are addicted to their public reputation than their children are plenty whereas transparent and sincere fathers who loves their children than their reputation are few. And that requires sacrifice which proves you are worthy of being the father of your child. Don't be one, if you cant be one of the sacrificers!*

### Fela Durotoye
*Many men have children, but not many children have 'Fathers'. Age releases to you reproductive skills. Fatherhood requires LEADERSHIP skills.*

*Real Fathers make a positive impact on their generation, and so give the next generation the advantage of a better nation to live in.*

*Real Fathers are Solution Providers and not a part of the problem to be solved.*

*Real Fathers are men of integrity & honour. Their word is their bond.*

*Real Fathers are Role Models worthy of emulation. They choose to live exemplary lifestyles of leadership and excellence*

### George Saunders
*He was a father. That's what a father does. Eases the burdens of those he loves. Saves the ones he loves from painful last images that might endure for a lifetime.*

### Hendrith Vanlon Smith Jr.
*As fathers, we know that our children need our love and need our guidance and need our faith in them. We know that our children need from us what only we as fathers can provide them.*

### Janvier Chouteu-Chando
*No true... father would be unconcerned about discord in his family that may cause it to disintegrate in his absence...*

### Jennifer Garner
*I am lucky to have had an attentive, curious and loving dad and heart-smart, down-to-earth, gifted mother. They changed the outlooks of their own lives and have never forgotten the people and organizations that helped them dream bigger than their circumstances should have allowed.*

### Joan Ambu
*Being a father is a choice. Staying true to fatherhood is a duty.*

### John Malkovich
*I'm more comfortable with whatever's wrong with me than my father was whenever he felt he failed or didn't measure up to the standard he set.*

### Johnny Knoxville
*I'm the fun dad, I am also the disciplinarian.*

### Jonathan Safran Foer
*When you're a dad, there's no one above you. If I don't do something that has to be done, who is going to do it?*

### Kent Nerburn
*It is much easier to become a father than to be one.*

### Michael Chabon
*You never would get through to the end of being a father, no matter where you stored your mind or how many steps in the series you followed. Not even if you died. Alive or dead a thousand miles distant, you were always going to be on the hook for work that was neither a procedure nor a series of steps but, rather, something that demanded your full, constant attention without necessarily calling you to do, perform, or say anything at all.*

### Mike Singletary
*If a dad does his job, we don't need prisons, we don't need jails. That's what I saw growing up.*

### Neil Kennedy
*There is no greater influence in the lives of your children than the words you speak over them. The blessing of the father is incredibly potent and powerful. Your words give your children potential. As their father, you are prophesying their future!*

### Paul Raeburn
*Fatherhood is about helping children become happy and healthy adults who are at ease in the world and prepared to become fathers or mothers themselves. We often say that doing what's best for our kids is more important than anything else we do. What's best for our kids should always include a role for fathers.*

### Richie Sambora
*You know, no matter what I am or what I do for a living, I'm still, you know, the husband and the dad and the protector of the house, and I have to be conscientious about that.*

### Tony Dungy
*But there's no substitute for a full-time dad. Dads who are fully engaged with their kids overwhelmingly tend to produce children who believe in themselves and live full lives.*

# *The Protection of Fathers*

### *Andrew Galasetti*
*Do whatever you must do to protect your children and wife.*

### *Burt Ward*
*I like to protect children. I mean, there's nothing wrong with having adult programming for mature adults that can selectively decide what they want to watch.*

### *Catherynne M. Valente*
*I abandoned her. It's the one capital crime of fatherhood. Mothers can fail a thousand different ways. A father's only job is: do not abandon this child.*

### *Charles Kettering*
*A father's protection is the greatest gift he can give to his children.*

### *David Beckham*
*A good father protects his children by setting boundaries and teaching them right from wrong.*

### *Eleesha*
*As a Father, I willingly nurture & protect the Soul's of all those - I love.*

### *Frederick Douglass*
*Fathers protect their children by being their first and strongest line of defense.*

### *Greg Gutfeld*
*We base communities on the idea of protecting children based on the sacrifice of adults.*

### Gregory David Roberts
*Nothing ever fits the palm so perfectly, or feels so right, or inspires so much protective instinct as the hand of a child.*

### Harlan Coben
*I look at the helpless bundle in the crib and she looks up at me and I wonder what I would notdo to protect her. I would lay down my life in a second. And truth be told, if push came to shove, I would lay down yours too.*

### Howard W. Hunter
*A righteous father protects his children with his time and presence.*

*To protect his children, a father must be present, involved, and attentive.*

### Ian Morgan Cron
*A father protects his children by teaching them to be brave and independent.*

### J. August Strindberg
*A father's duty is to protect his children from the dangers of the world.*

### James T. Walsh
*The Children's Safety Act will help protect children from the perpetrators of these vile crimes.*

### John Green
*To protect his children, a father must be strong in character and gentle in spirit.*

**Leo Buscaglia**
*Fathers protect their children not just physically, but emotionally and spiritually as well.*

**Leo Buscaglia**
*If there is any immortality to be had among us human beings, it is certainly only in the love that we leave behind. Fathers like mine don't ever die.*

**Plato**
*The best way of training the young is to train yourself at the same time; not to admonish them, but to be seen never doing that of which you would admonish them.*

**Ralph Moody**
*Son, there are times a man has to do things he doesn't like to, in order to protect his family.*

**Sigmund Freud**
*I cannot think of any need in childhood as strong as the need for a father's protection.*

**Theodore Roosevelt**
*The greatest protection a father can offer is a safe and loving home.*

**Thornton Wilder**
*It wasn't our love that protected them—it was that promise.*

**Tom Wolfe**
*Sherman made the terrible discovery that men make about their fathers sooner or later... that his child would have something mythical and infinitely important: a Protector, who would keep a lid on all the chaotic and catastrophic possibilities of life.*

# *Parenting*

**Amy Sherman-Palladino**
*I grew up where my parents would literally shove me in the car rather than have to say hello to a neighbor.*

**Anne Frank**
*How true Daddy's words were when he said: all children must look after their own upbringing. Parents can only give good advice or put them on the right paths, but the final forming of a person's character lies in their own hands.*

**Augustus Hare**
*Love, it has been said, flows downward. The love of parents for their children has always been far more powerful than that of children for their parents and who among the sons of men ever loved God with a thousandth part of the love which God has manifested to us?*

**Barack Obama**
*My parents shared not only an improbable love, they shared an abiding faith in the possibilities of this nation. They would give me an African name, Barack, or blessed, believing that in a tolerant America your name is no barrier to success.*

**Ben Stein**
*Screaming at children over their grades, especially to the point of the child's tears, is child abuse, pure and simple. It's not funny and it's not good parenting. It is a crushing, scarring, disastrous experience for the child. It isn't the least bit funny.*

**Benjamin Carson**
*People spending more of their own money on routine health care would make the system more competitive and transparent and restore the confidence between the patients and the doctors without government rationing.*

**Candace Bushnell**
*My parents had a great marriage. Interestingly, it made it harder for me in relationships because I knew what a good relationship looked like.*

**Caroline Kennedy**
*Education was the most important value in our home when I was growing up. People don't always realize that my parents shared a sense of intellectual curiosity and a love of reading and of history.*

**Cat Cora**
*I believe that parents need to make nutrition education a priority in their home environment. It's crucial for good health and longevity to instill in your children sound eating habits from an early age.*

༻ ༺

*When I'm home, the heart and soul of our family is in the kitchen. Growing up, my parents both worked, so dinnertime was for family - the TV was off. I think it's important to grab that time and really make it special, even after a tough day.*

**Dan Savage**
*The bullied straight kid goes home to a shoulder to cry on and support and can talk freely about his experience at school and why he's being bullied. I couldn't go home and open up to my parents.*

**Daniel Goleman**
*Emotional intelligence begins to develop in the earliest years. All the small exchanges children have with their parents, teachers, and with each other carry emotional messages.*

### Dennis Prager
*From their teenage years on, children are considerably more capable of causing parents unhappiness than bringing them happiness. That is one reason parents who rely on their children for happiness make both their children and themselves miserable.*

### Diana Ross
*I'm a parent, and I try to take care of my health and keep my life in order. In the last few years I've really had to decide what's important to me, and it seems to me that my family and my health are top on the list. And those have nothing to do with show business.*

### Dixie Carter
*Learning can take place in the backyard if there is a human being there who cares about the child. Before learning computers, children should learn to read first. They should sit around the dinner table and hear what their parents have to say and think.*

### Donal Logue
*It was all that stuff about taking your parents' car when you're 13, sneaking booze into rock shows and ditching school with your friends. I could relate to that as a former teenager, rather than as a present parent.*

### Drew Barrymore
*You can't live your life blaming your failures on your parents and what they did or didn't do for you. You're dealt the cards that you're dealt. I realised it was a waste of time to be angry at my parents and feel sorry for myself.*

### Elizabeth Gilbert
*Nobody until very recently would have thought that their husband was supposed to be their best friend, confidante, intellectual soul mate, co-parent, inspiration.*

### Emily Mortimer
*I'm still shy - I'm no good at my children's parent-teacher conferences, and I'm slowly learning how to ask for what I want. But I now know that I have a reserve of courage to draw upon when I really need it. There's nothing that I'm too scared to have a go at.*

### Emmylou Harris
*My parents were not very happy. They were very worried about me pursuing a career that even if I had talent might not give me the happiness and the success that they - any parent hopes for their child.*

### Ernest Istook
*Education begins at home and I applaud the parents who recognize that they - not someone else - must take responsibility to assure that their children are well educated.*

### Frank Pittman
*Each generation's job is to question what parents accept on faith, to explore possibilities, and adapt the last generation's system of values for a new age.*

### Gail Porter
*My parents' marriage was very rocky. They were always arguing. When they split up when I was in my 20s, my brother and I were both delighted because we knew they weren't good for each other.*

### George Bernard Shaw
*Parentage is a very important profession, but no test of fitness for it is ever imposed in the interest of the children.*

### George Santayana
*Parents lend children their experience and a vicarious memory children endow their parents with a vicarious immortality.*

### Heidi Klum
*I think if you give your best as a parent, then that's all you can do.*

### Henry Ward Beecher
*We never know the love of a parent till we become parents ourselves.*

### Herbert Spencer
*The wise man must remember that while he is a descendant of the past, he is a parent of the future.*

### Horace
*Suffering is but another name for the teaching of experience, which is the parent of instruction and the schoolmaster of life.*

### Jennifer Garner
*I'm still really close with everyone at home and their parents - and their brothers and sisters. I was so, so, so lucky to grow up as part of a community and I don't take that for granted. I try very hard to stay part of it.*

### Jhumpa Lahiri
*I don't know why, but the older I get the more interested I get in my parents' marriage. And it's interesting to be married yourself, too, because there is an inevitable comparison.*

### Joan Cusack
*I take parenting incredibly seriously. I want to be there for my kids and help them navigate the world, and develop skills, emotional intelligence, to enjoy life, and I'm lucky to be able to do that and have two healthy, normal boys.*

**John Mahoney**
*I took the fear of marriage from my parents' relationship, because I didn't want to end up in a relationship like that, whereas my brothers and sisters learnt a lesson from it and made sure they didn't carry it on into their own marriages.*

**Kyle Chandler**
*My grandparents got married at a very young age, and a lot of what I think about marriage is based on their relationship. I watched them over the years and saw how they dealt with everything together, as a team.*

**L.R. Knost**
*Parenting has nothing to do with perfection. Perfection isn't even the goal, not for us, not for our children. Learning together to live well in an imperfect world, loving each other despite or even because of our imperfections, and growing as humans while we grow our little humans, those are the goals of gentle parenting. So don't ask yourself at the end of the day if you did everything right. Ask yourself what you learned and how well you loved, then grow from your answer. That is perfect parenting.*

*We don't lose ourselves in parenthood. We find parts of ourselves we never knew existed.*

*When we encourage new parents to 'treasure these moments because they don't last forever' we need to remember to also reassure them that they will survive these moments because they don't last forever. Parenting is hard, and the struggles can sometimes feel like they overshadow the joys. Knowing that struggling is normal and will pass helps us get through the hard times so we can truly treasure the good ones.*

*Children need to know that they matter, that someone in this big, scary, beautiful world thinks that they are the sun, moon, and stars all rolled into one lovable little human. The world will hurt and disillusion them at times, no doubt, but knowing that they are loved beyond measure by someone who's got their back, knowing they are not alone, knowing they always have arms to run to when they're hurt or afraid, will help them to pick themselves up and move on, again and again and again.*

### Laura Schlessinger
*Children are our second chance to have a great parent-child relationship.*

### LeBron James
*But now, being a parent, I go home and see my son and I forget about any mistake I ever made or the reason I'm upset. I get home and my son is smiling or he comes running to me. It has just made me grow as an individual and grow as a man.*

### Liza Minnelli
*You see, that's another thing that my parents gave me: an enormously great sense of humor.*

### Marian Wright Edelman
*Parents have become so convinced that educators know what is best for their children that they forget that they themselves are really the experts.*

### Max Irons
*Acting advice is a bit like your parents teaching you how to drive a car. You know they're right, but you still kind of want them to shut up a bit.*

**Michael Ian Black**

*There is no word for feeling nostalgic about the future, but that's what a parent's tears often are, a nostalgia for something that has not yet occurred. They are the pain of hope, the helplessness of hope, and finally, the surrender to hope.*

**Mika Brzezinski**

*I realize that of all people, I am no expert on parenting or marriage.*

**Mindy Kaling**

*I think a lot of writers, male and female, write as if their parents were killed in a car accident when they were 2, and they have no one to hold accountable. And unfortunately, I don't have that. I have parents who I care about what they think.*

**Oliver Hudson**

*Father or stepfather - those are just titles to me. They don't mean anything.*

**Olivia Williams**

*My parents' long and happy marriage was a great ideal to live up to, but a tough one.*

**Phil McGraw**

*The Internet is just bringing all kinds of information into the home. There's just a lot of distraction, a lot of competition for the parent's voice to resonate in the children's ears.*

**Princess Diana**

*I think like any marriage, especially when you've had divorced parents like myself you want to try even harder to make it work.*

### Regina King
*I learned a lot from my Mom. My favorite lesson: remember there is no such thing as a certain way to parent and to remember that you are learning along with your child - it's ok to make mistakes.*

### Rita Dove
*My father is a chemist, my mother was a homemaker. My parents instilled in us the feeling that learning was the most exciting thing that could happen to you, and it never ends.*

### Robert Neelly Bellah
*However painful the process of leaving home, for parents and for children, the really frightening thing for both would be the prospect of the child never leaving home.*

### Roger Moore
*Teach love, generosity, good manners and some of that will drift from the classroom to the home and who knows, the children will be educating the parents.*

### Shirley Henderson
*Children don't just play any more - they're far too busy learning to fence and taking extra French classes. In the end, you're actually doing more damage to your children by trying to hot-house them. It's far better to remain a calm parent.*

### Trevor Noah
*People say all the time that they'd do anything for the people they love. But would you really? Would you do anything? Would you give everything? I don't know that a child knows that kind of selfless love. A mother, yes. A mother will clutch her children and jump from a moving car to keep them from harm. She will do it without thinking. But I don't think the child knows how to do that, not instinctively. It's something the child has to learn.*

### Tsultrim Allione

*As I cooked in the cauldron of motherhood, the incredible love I felt for my children opened my heart and brought me a much greater understanding of universal love. It made me understand the suffering of the world much more deeply.*

### Vanessa Diffenbaugh

*She was perfect. I knew this the moment she emerged from my body, white and wet and wailing. Beyond the requisite ten fingers and ten toes, the beating heart, the lungs inhaling and exhaling oxygen, my daughter knew how to scream. She knew how to make herself heard. She knew how to reach out and latch on. She knew what she needed to do to survive. I didn't know how it was possible that such perfection could have developed within a body as flawed as my own, but when I looked into her face, I saw that it clearly was.*

### Veronika Jensen

*You and I. Hand in hand. An endless story of love. A love that grew in me for 9 months and only grows bigger each day. You and I. Hand in hand. An endless journey. Countless steps. One destination - your happiness. You and I. Hand in hand. My heart and blood. I'll share it all - take it - my whole life is you.*

### Victor LaValle

*"That's the funny thing," she said. "Men always want to die for something. For someone. I can see the appeal. You do it once and it's done. No more worrying, not knowing, about tomorrow and tomorrow and tomorrow. I know you all think it sounds brave, but I'll tell you something even braver. To struggle and fight for the ones you love today. And then do it all over again the next day. Every day. For your whole life. It's not as romantic, I admit. But it takes a lot of courage to live for someone, too.*

### Vimala McClure
*A wise mother knows: It is her state of consciousness that matters. Her gentleness and clarity command respect. Her love creates security.*

*Children are mirrors; they will always show you exactly what is going on inside of you. Each phase of their growth is an opportunity to heal your own pain, to go deeper inside yourself and become more truly human.*

### Virginie Despentes
*In much the same way, motherhood has become the essential female experience, valued above all others: giving life is where it's at.*

### Vivek Thangaswamy
*Every woman is a gift when she becomes a daughter, Every woman is beautiful when she becomes a lover, Every woman is special when she becomes a wife, Every woman is a god when she becomes a Mother.*

### Warwick Davis
*My parents armed me with an amazing sense of humor, and it's what you need when, well, it's what anyone needs in this world.*

### Yogi Berra
*Little League baseball is a very good thing because it keeps the parents off the streets*

### Yrsa Daley-Ward

*This fettered concept of motherhood is outdated. You can go and come back and go and come back and I shall always be here. I shall always be here. That is real Love for you, and don't let anyone tell you any different.*

### Zadie Smith

*You don't have favourites among your children, but you do have allies.*

### Victor Devlin

*Listen, there is no way any true man is going to let children live around him in his home and not discipline and teach, fight and mold them until they know all he knows. His goal is to make them better than he is. Being their friend is a distant second to this.*

*I hope you have enjoyed this.*

**If you have,**
**please leave me a review on Amazon.**

*And check out some more in the series*
*(more being added all the time!)*

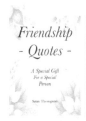

# *About the Author*

Sean has done a lot since his days of picking fruit in southern British Columbia and planting trees in northern Alberta and Manitoba; landscaping, line-cooking, performing at weekly ceremonies in Tokyo and, what he now considers to be his double-edged true calling, teaching children and adults how to be creative with technology and authoring books.

Sean is an educational technology specialist at an international school in Tokyo. He has traveled extensively speaking, presenting and participating in discussions regarding the effective integration of technology in an educational setting.

Made in United States
Cleveland, OH
09 December 2024